OLIVER LANSLEY

Oliver Lansley has worked extensively in theatre, establishing Les Enfants Terribles Theatre Company (www.lesenfantsterribles. co.uk) in 2002 with their first production *West* (Assembly Rooms, Edinburgh; winner of the Herald Devil Award). Les Enfants Terribles has returned to every successive Edinburgh Festival with the following productions: *The Germinator* (2003; winner of Hairline Highlight Award); *Bedtime Stories* (2004); and *Immaculate* (2005).

Oliver has written a number of other plays, has had his work showcased by the BBC, and in 2005 was invited onto the Royal Court Young Writers' Programme. He is also currently working on several television projects with his production company, Room 5 Productions (www.room5productions.com), most notably *FM* for Channel 4 in which he co-stars.

Oliver is also an established actor, having performed in many theatre productions ranging from Eddy in Berkoff's *Greek* at Riverside Studios, to the award-winning one-man show, *The Germinator*. His film and TV credits include *Holby City*, *Doctors, EastEnders* and numerous other television productions and short films for the likes of Cinema Extreme, the NFTS and the British Council.

Other Titles by Nick Hern Books

Oliver Lansley

IMMACULATE

NICK HERN BOOKS
London
www.nickhernbooks.co.uk

A Nick Hern Book

Immaculate first published in Great Britain as a paperback original in 2006 by Nick Hern Books Limited, 14 Larden Road, London W3 7ST

Reprinted 2008, 2009, 2010, 2011, 2012

Immaculate copyright © 2006 Oliver Lansley

Oliver Lansley has asserted his right to be identified as the author of this work

Cover design: Oliver Lansley

Typeset by Country Setting, Kingsdown, Kent CT14 8ES
Printed in the UK by Mimeo Ltd, Huntingdon, Cambridgeshire PE29 6XX

A CIP catalogue record for this book is available from the British Library

ISBN   978 1 85459 944 5

Introduction

Having something published for the first time is an incredible
thrill for any writer. You feel like finally there will be a small
piece of your work etched in stone for all eternity that can
never be removed. Slightly overdramatic perhaps but nevertheless very exciting!

Having this particular play published has been especially
rewarding because of the way it all came about. Many young
playwrights assume that the only way they will ever see their
work in print is if it gets picked up by one of the major new
writing theatres in town. These theatre companies do fantastic
work; however, for people whose desire it is to create theatre
beyond merely submitting a script, it can be quite frustrating
and limiting.

The pleasure of having *Immaculate* published is that it took a
different route. I wrote, directed and produced the show with
my own theatre company, Les Enfants Terribles, which I
established in 2002 to produce new work. I managed to drag it
up to the Edinburgh Festival with little money, a lot of faith
and a lot of favours. Now to have the piece recognised in this
way and for it to be embarking on a tour is a real privilege, and
I hope it will encourage others like me, who have a real
enthusiasm for creating theatre, that you can achieve these
things purely through hard work and blind determination.
Admittedly, it may take a bit longer, be a lot more work and at
times, a lot more frustrating, but if and when you do get there,
I promise it is a lot more satisfying!

So, to anyone out there who has a passion for making theatre
and is stuck performing in some dingy cave in the annals of
Edinburgh somewhere to two drunken audience members and a
friendly member of the front-of-house staff, keep it up. We
need people like you to be producing new theatre, writing new
work, talking about new things. As excellent as the new-writing
theatre industry is at the moment, nothing can compare to the

people who are spending all their time, money and energy trying to create something new in the theatre and trying to say something they think is important. That is what is exciting about the theatre, what pushes the medium forward. I sincerely hope that this small victory will encourage others to keep plugging away and working too hard and throwing all their money away into the seemingly bottomless pit of theatre production. It can be worth it in the end.

Acknowledgements

Firstly, my incredible parents without whom I would have and be nothing, and there is no way in the world I would have been able to achieve even a fraction of what I have done, thank you, thank you, thank you and I love you. Also to Kate Winn, a remarkable woman for whom I have a great deal of love and respect – thank you for everything. Iain Harvey, a man who has shown blind faith in me and contributed to my last two Edinburgh shows, despite losing money! I should probably stop before this turns into a gushing Oscar-acceptance speech but thanks also to the Gilded Balloon; to all the venues who have been involved in the tour of *Immaculate*; the cast and crew; to the wonderful Ex Amino; founding members of Les Enfants Terribles – boys, I am privileged to count two such geniuses as friends; James Seager, another who has been there from the start working for no thanks and no money – thank you, mate. My lovely agent Jess at David Higham Associates, Nick Hern Books and anyone else who has helped me out. Thank you – I do appreciate it and also to anyone else who has actually read right through to the end of this ridiculously long acknowledgments list – thank you too, I hope you enjoy the play.

OLIVER LANSLEY

Immaculate was first performed by Les Enfants Terribles Theatre Company as part of the 2005 Edinburgh Festival Fringe, at the Gilded Balloon, Edinburgh, on 3 August 2005. The cast was as follows:

MIA	Melanie Gray
GABRIEL	Christopher Mellows
LUCIFER	Matt Ian Kelly
MICHAEL	James Seager
REBECCA	Nicole Lewis
GARY GOODMAN	Oliver Lansley

Director   Oliver Lansley
Stage/Tour Manager   James Mathews
Sound/Visual Design   Ex Animo Productions

The production was revived at The Space, London on 2 March 2006, and subsequently at the Corn Exchange, Wallingford; the Wycombe Swan, High Wycombe; the Arena Theatre, Wolverhampton; Reigate Grammar and Oxted Country School, Surrey; the Old Red Lion, London; Croft Hall, Hungerford; Marlborough Theatre, Brighton; and Streetwise Fringe, Dubai. The cast was as follows:

MIA	Sarah Kirkland
GABRIEL	Christopher Mellows
LUCIFER	Matt Ian Kelly
MICHAEL	James Seager
REBECCA	Claire Westwood
GARY GOODMAN	Timothy Edwin Brown

Director   Oliver Lansley
Stage/Tour Manager   James Mathews
Sound/Visual Design   Ex Animo Productions

IMMACULATE

Characters

MIA, *twenty/thirty-something*

REBECCA, *Mia's best friend*

MICHAEL, *Mia's ex-boyfriend*

GABRIEL, *an Archangel*

LUCIFER, *a Fallen Angel*

GARY GOODMAN, *Mia's old classmate*

CHORUS

The action takes place in Mia's small bedsit.

On stage are two chairs, a hatstand and a Greek column on which sits a phone. There is a door stage right (the front door to the flat) and a door stage left (the door to the rest of the flat). It is recommended to use actual doors wherever possible, as opposed to just the wings, for maximum comic effect. If actual doors are unavailable for the production, most entrances can be performed offstage, as if in the hallway.

. . . can represent the trailing off of a sentence, a pause or the line being interrupted.

ACT ONE

The scene is set with dramatic music. A Classical Greek
CHORUS, *dressed in black and wearing masks, enter. (Note:*
the CHORUS *are played by the actors who portray*
MICHAEL, GABRIEL, LUCIFER *and* REBECCA.)

The CHORUS *speak. They physicalise each action with a*
succinct and precise movement; it should be slick and stylised.

CHORUS.
Upon this stage a tale we bring to you
Of devils, angels, infants and a womb
The womb of whom upon our story rests
A female, young, with fire in her breast
Her life, not one of solitude but vice
Indulgence presiding over sacrifice.
Yet still her form was chosen as the host
To a child whose being mattered more than most.
Her unasked task was just to incubate
A child they say had greatness as his fate
But prepared for such a role our muse was not
And less than happy was she with her lot
And added to this growing mount of fear
The father of said child was less than clear.
A claim is staked from dark and one from light
And one from mortal, present on the night
And so begins our tale with her reception
Of the unexpected news of its conception.

The CHORUS *exit and a single light comes up on a phone*
which sits on a column. As the light comes up, the phone
begins to ring. After a moment, a voice shouts from offstage.

MIA (*offstage*). Fuck off.

She continues to curse at the ringing phone from offstage. A
toilet flushes as lights come up on a small room. It is
functional with little in it.

The phone continues to ring persistently as MIA *continues to shout abuse at it from offstage.*

Fuck off . . . I'm coming . . . Alright . . . OK . . . hang on for Christ's sake!

MIA *bursts onto the stage. She is clearly heavily pregnant and dressed in comfortable tracksuit-style clothes. She is holding a pregnancy test. She answers the phone. She is slightly frantic.*

WHAT?

Yes . . . YES, I've just done it . . .

I've got it here . . .

I'm looking at it now . . .

Well, it doesn't say anything yet . . .

I don't know how long . . . five minutes?

She picks up the home-pregnancy-test instructions and reads the back.

The pack just says a few . . .

Well, I don't know . . . three . . . ?

She disregards the instructions.

This is ridiculous . . .

I can't be – it's not possible . . .

No literally . . .

Biologically . . .

No . . . *literally*, I *literally* haven't had sex since Michael . . .

I know . . .

I KNOW . . .

Well, there's definitely something in there . . .

I can feel it moving around . . .

So how do you explain the massive fucking bulge I'm hiding under my sister's jumper?

. . . Because my sister is fatter than me and my jumpers won't fit . . .

. . . Yes, I'm sure it's not just gas . . .

Looking at watch.

Three and a half . . .

OK . . .

She stares at the test.

I can see something . . .

Something's happening . . .

It's a line . . .

It's a blue line . . .

What the fuck does a blue line mean?

She desperately fishes around for the instructions and reads them frantically. Suddenly she stops moving and stares forward.

. . . I'm pregnant.

Fuck.

She puts the phone down.

Beat.

(*To audience.*) That was my friend Rebecca on the phone, she's three years younger than me and has never had a boyfriend for more than seven months . . .

The idea of having children abhors her, she says the mere thought of a small, bald, wrinkly human being crawling out of her delicate feminine area is enough to make her avoid sex for ever . . .

She has nightmares about it . . .

Fields of hundreds of tiny babies with the faces of her mother and father, all screaming at her and shitting their pants, while she runs around desperately to try and change their nappies, but the cycle of shitting is so constant from the many, many babies, she can never keep up and there is a constant stench and never-ending, screeching howls from the many soiled, screaming, wrinkly little monsters . . .

At this point she wakes up in tears, covered in a damp sweat and rings me . . .

Who is always fast asleep, to say . . .

She picks up the phone. REBECCA *appears in the doorway upstage left, holding a phone, shrieking.*

REBECCA. I had it again, those little bastards won't leave me alone . . . I can't bear it . . . the stench, the screams, the dead, shark eyes of my mother laughing at me as she shits all over my . . .

MIA. Calm down, you don't have to have children . . .

You're on the pill, you use condoms, you're protected, have a bloody hysterectomy if you want, then you know you're safe . . .

It *is* a preventative problem, they don't just appear in your womb from nowhere, demanding to be bred.

She puts the phone down, REBECCA *exits.* MIA *turns back to the audience.*

Well, they don't . . .

At least that was my understanding . . .

But this isn't about Rebecca, this is about me . . .

Who is, as you can see, pregnant, heavily.

Now, I don't have Rebecca's inherent fear of babies, I don't mind babies; in fact, I'd even go as far to say I actually quite like babies, and I probably did intend to have one . . .

At some point,

Or at least I assumed I would,

At some point,

When I was happily married in my own house, with a gingham apron . . .

And an Aga and . . .

A dog . . .

I don't have any of those things . . .

But I am pregnant, heavily . . .

Which is odd to say the least.

You see, I haven't actually had sex since I broke up with my ex, Michael.

. . . He claimed that we were both 'changing, but we weren't allowing each other to move on, that everything else in our lives was progressing but we were forcing each other to stay as the people we knew, which apparently weren't the people that we were any more . . . '

. . .

Which is bollocks, HE was changing and the new HIM wanted to be single . . . Prick.

MICHAEL *suddenly bursts through the door upstage left.*

MICHAEL. God, you're so unreasonable, see this is why . . . this is what happens . . . you're the only person that can make me like this, I'm not like this any more.

MIA. What? No, Michael, I'm not the only person who makes you like *this*, I'm the only person you show *this* to because I'm the person you take all your shit out on. Because you've given up trying to 'impress' me.

MICHAEL. That's bollocks!

MIA. It is not bollocks, the *new* Michael wouldn't be so laid back if he didn't use me to take out all his fucking issues . . .

MICHAEL. You're such a fucking martyr, MAYBE this isn't about YOU, maybe this is about ME.

MIA. Oh, I'm absolutely positive it's about YOU, it's always about YOU, that's the only thing YOU understand.

MICHAEL. WHAT? My God, you're impossible, I can't even talk to you any more, you won't allow yourself to be spoken to, you treat me like the person you *assume* I am, which is not the person I am any more.

MIA. Oh really, you've 'moved on' . . . ?

MICHAEL. Yes.

MIA. NO, Michael, you may *think* you've moved on but you're in exactly the same place, having exactly the same arguments and being exactly the same dickhead you've always been.

MICHAEL. NO I'M NOT, I'm a different dickhead, a dickhead you don't know any more. You don't know me, you don't know the ME any more.

MIA. I do know the YOU, Michael, in fact I'm probably the only person who does know YOU properly, Michael, and that's your problem. You don't like to be reminded of that fact and you can't pretend to be 'wonderful new Michael' because I know it's BULLSHIT!

MICHAEL. God, you're a dick! DICK!

MIA. Oh yes, NOW I see the new mature Michael. God, you're so right, I was so mistaken. Who is this wonderful new man standing before me?

MICHAEL. Fuck off, FUCK OFF!

MIA. Brilliant Michael, brilliant.

MICHAEL. FUUUUUCK YOU!

He walks out and slams the door. (Note: if possible have MICHAEL *exit through the audience.)*

MIA. DICK! . . .

(*Calmly, to the audience.*) . . . and so now we are no longer together . . .

But that's irrelevant . . .

The relevant part is that *that* – (*Referencing the argument we just saw.*) happened well over nine months ago,

And Michael is the last person I had sex with . . .

And as you can probably guess we didn't have sex for at least the last month and a half of us being together . . .

So . . .

My condition is . . . somewhat puzzling . . .

I'm pregnant . . .

I'm fucking pregnant, heavily,

In here there is a small person curled up in the foetal position, breathing through his belly button, sitting in a big bag of piss waiting to rule my life,

That's weird, isn't it . . . ?

She looks down at her stomach.

There's someone in there . . . in that little bump . . .

A little person with the potential to become anything . . .

A little person that *I'm* responsible for,

A life, that I'm responsible for . . .

I can't even take care of myself, my own life is hardly a picture of perfection . . .

How am I supposed to guide anyone else through theirs?

Parents know everything, can do everything, have the answers to anything . . .

I can't even remember to water my plants for goodness' sake, what will I do . . . ?

God help me . . .

There is a knock at the door. MIA looks confused then looks down at her watch. Suddenly she remembers something and panics.

Shit, shit, shit! I totally forgot . . . bear with me one second.

She goes over and opens the door, hiding her bump and tracksuit behind it. A man, GABRIEL, stands in the doorway.

GABRIEL. Hello . . .

MIA. Ah, hello . . . Look, I'm afraid I'm not going to be able to see you today . . . something has come up . . .

GABRIEL. I . . . oh er . . . you were expecting me then?

MIA. Of course I was, it slipped my mind, I'm terribly sorry but . . . if you call me to reschedule, then . . .

GABRIEL. Right . . . well, it's just I've come an awfully long way . . .

MIA. . . . Right.

GABRIEL. I mean a really long way, maybe if I could just come in for a moment, it won't take much time . . .

She looks at him and sighs.

MIA. One second . . .

She shuts the door again and turns back to the audience.

As she speaks, she swiftly whips off her comfortable tracksuit garb, and pulls on a chic sexy dress – wrestling it over the bump.

OK look, there's a little something I haven't told you yet . . . It's not a big deal, it's just that sometimes people can get a bit put off by it and . . . well, look, I don't want you to get the wrong impression . . . It's just people have all these preconceptions which are usually way off the mark . . . and well . . . look, just don't get all judgemental on me . . . OK?

She opens the door. GABRIEL is still standing there looking confused.

Right, come in, put your stuff on the bed, get undressed and I will be with you in two ticks.

GABRIEL. I . . .

She ignores him and turns to us. GABRIEL stares at her.

Throughout the entire next section up to ' . . . I won't be long', we witness the dramatic transformation of MIA from frumpy tracksuit to sleek and vampy mistress, complete with hair, make-up and 'fuck me' boots. The transformation

should be slick and choreographed almost like a dance and
MIA*'s focus should be on her delivery as opposed to her*
props.

Once GABRIEL *is in the room,* MIA *needs pay no attention*
to him. She can even get him to hold her make-up mirror,
for instance, and lean on him to get herself ready; she is not
put off by his presence.

MIA. OK . . . So I am what you would call 'a lady of the
night', a mistress, a madam, a dominatrix.

Let me make this clear: I am *not* a whore. I do not actually
have sex with these people, in fact a lot of the stuff I do is
pretty un-sexual. For instance, there's this one chap that
comes over, I blindfold him, tie him up, go shopping for a
couple of hours, come back, untie him and he pays me two
hundred quid!

Don't get me wrong, they're not all quite as vanilla, there's
the odd hand job here and there, and there's this merchant
banker from Hertfordshire that comes round once a month
and gives me £500 to cum in my hair, but on the whole it's
fairly genial.

I am aware though this does change the context a little bit,
but what I said earlier about not having sex since Michael,
that is all absolutely true . . .

GABRIEL. Excuse me, miss . . .

MIA. Just pop your clothes off and wash yourself in the sink if
you need to . . .

Look, I've never been a fan of menial work, I've worked in
shops, restaurants, offices and I hated it. Basically, this is
just a way of making a lot of money for not a lot of work,
I would have considered pole dancing but I just don't have
the upper-body strength . . .

It's just business really, a job like any other, which is why I
didn't mention this to you before, because I didn't want you
to get involved in all those stereotypes of me being some
sort of crack whore or something ridiculous like that. It
really is a lot more wholesome than that. I mean, I know a

pregnant mistress doesn't conjure up great images but really it's . . . I have a very normal homely life . . .

GABRIEL. Miss?

MIA. Keep it in your trousers for one more second, you're not being charged, there are magazines in the drawer if you want them . . .

Look, I'm not going to make excuses for it. Put it this way, I work on average five hours a week and at this rate I'll have paid off my mortgage in the next three years . . . So that's that, I'm glad we've got it all out in the open.

She looks over at GABRIEL *and sighs.*

Right . . . well, I suppose I should get this over with . . . I won't be long.

She grabs a riding crop from the hatstand in the corner of the room and descends on GABRIEL *who, terrified, shuffles out of her path.*

GABRIEL. Look, I think there's been some mistake.

I'm here for the baby?

MIA (*sighing*). . . . If you go through there you can change, there are nappies and romper suits in the cupboard, pink or blue, you're probably an extra large . . .

GABRIEL (*pointing to her stomach*). No . . . *your* baby.

MIA *glares at him.*

MIA. Excuse me?

GABRIEL. Your baby?

MIA (*taken aback*). Sorry, what are you trying to . . . ?

He pulls a scroll out of his pocket and shows it to MIA.

GABRIEL. That is your name, correct?

MIA. Yes.

GABRIEL. And the details are correct, date of birth and so forth?

MIA. Yes, how did you . . . ?

GABRIEL. Right, so then, it's one of ours.

MIA. Sorry? Ours? What? What are you talking about? Who is ours? Who are you?

GABRIEL. Oh goodness, sorry, I should introduce myself. We have a policy for this usually, as obviously it's a stressful situation but . . . look, I've been travelling all day, and then I get here and you ask me to take my clothes off and . . .

MIA. Who are you?

GABRIEL. I'm Gabriel, I'm an angel, *the* angel. The baby . . . it's one of ours.

MIA *stares at him blankly.*

Maybe you should sit down, I know it can be quite a shock.

MIA *sits, she is a little stunned.*

MIA. What? So . . . you're telling me this baby is . . .

GABRIEL. One of the divine, a lamb of God, a child of creation . . .

MIA. I . . . ? But why would . . . ?

GABRIEL. . . . I'm assuming you've heard of the second coming? It has been prophesied for quite some time now.

MIA. Hang on, SECOND coming? What . . . ? So Jesus is being reincarnated in my . . . ?

GABRIEL. No, no, no, we don't do 'reincarnation'.

MIA (*confused*). Oh, so how would you describe this then?

GABRIEL. The second coming.

MIA. Right, just with different words then . . . forgive me for being difficult but why should I believe you? Have you got any proof?

GABRIEL. I'm afraid we don't do proof . . . negates the whole faith thing.

MIA. Convenient . . . not even a little miracle? You know, water into wine sort of thing. I could do with a drink . . .

GABRIEL. I don't think that's wise . . . not with the baby . . .

MIA. Well, have you got any identification I can see?

GABRIEL. What sort of identification?

MIA. I don't know, some sort of licence maybe . . .

GABRIEL. Er . . .

MIA. What about wings, where are your wings?

GABRIEL. . . . I don't have them with me.

MIA. Right . . .

GABRIEL. Look, do you have any better explanation?

MIA (*looking down at the bump, realising she doesn't*). Well, no . . . not yet but . . .

GABRIEL. Then you're just going to have to take my word for it.

MIA. But . . .

GABRIEL. Oh, come on, you must have had some idea. I mean, the conception was immaculate, was it not?

MIA. Well, it was . . . *OK*, I suppose . . . I mean, you do know that I'm not a virgin?

GABRIEL. Yes, well, I was getting that impression.

Beat.

Ah well, who is these days? The important thing is that it's definitely one of ours. I mean, have you had any . . . ?

MIA. Any?

GABRIEL. . . . In the last nine months?

MIA. Sex?

GABRIEL. Sex . . . in the last nine months?

MIA. Not the sort of sex that's going to get me pregnant, no . . .

GABRIEL. I see, well, good, then it must be one of ours . . .

I suppose reformed is the new sinless these days. You're like a refurbished house, it doesn't matter if we didn't like the previous occupant's colour scheme, what matters now is that we've cleaned you up, put neutral colours throughout and your market price has risen again . . .

MIA. OK . . .

She takes a deep breath to steady herself.

So this is *your* baby?

GABRIEL. Well, not mine, no . . . you could say . . . it was God's baby.

MIA. Right . . .

She gathers her thoughts.

So . . . will God be paying child support?

GABRIEL. Excuse me?

MIA. I mean, what you're basically saying is that God picked me as a surrogate mother, without my permission I might add, to carry his child?

GABRIEL. Well . . .

MIA. . . . So what sort of contact will God be having with 'his' child. I mean, his presence isn't exactly a physical one, is it?

He's not the sort of father who can take his child to playgroup or put together his cot, is he?

GABRIEL. Well, we do know a carpenter . . .

MIA. . . . He's not going to be around to get up at four in the morning and change a nappy, is he?

GABRIEL. God will offer His constant love and support . . .

MIA. Right, but that's not going to buy the little fella a new pram, is it?

Or clean the sick off my suede boots?

. . . Unless *you're* coming to live with me?

GABRIEL. No.

MIA. No, so basically, he's just turned me into an X-year-old single mum then?

GABRIEL. Well . . .

MIA. Marvellous, fucking marvellous! Thank you, God!

GABRIEL. Well, He does move in mysterious ways.

MIA. Don't even give me that shit . . .

GABRIEL. Now just calm down . . .

MIA. Calm down? You come in here, no warning, no wings, telling me that I've just been impregnated by the almighty with not so much as a 'Hello, would you mind if I just . . . ?' I mean, what sort of way is that to treat the mother of your child? What happened to dinner and the movies first?

. . . And not even having the courtesy to tell me himself, just sending down some oafish lapdog to do his dirty work for him, some useless old . . .

GABRIEL (*exploding*). Now look here, lady! I've had a long journey, I'm tired, I'm stressed, I came down here to try and help you, shed some light on your situation and all you're giving me is grief. For goodness' sake, don't shoot the messenger . . . JESUS CHRIST!

They both look at each other in shock at such an outburst, GABRIEL *looks up nervously.*

There is an awkward pause.

Suddenly they both speak, breaking the silence apologetically.

MIA. . . . I'm sorry.

GABRIEL. . . . No, I'm sorry.

MIA. . . . I'm hormonal . . . ?

GABRIEL. . . . I shouldn't have snapped at you.

MIA. You're not oafish . . .

GABRIEL. Look, I understand it must be a bit of a shock. I'm just . . . you know . . .

MIA. I know . . . look, I'm sure it's not your fault.

GABRIEL. Well, no, it's not, but I'm always the one who has to deliver the news, good old Gabriel. You know, it doesn't mean that I necessarily agree with it, not saying I don't but . . .

It's hard, you know, you don't know me, like you say, you're a single girl, doing your own thing, you don't just want some mystery baby turning up in your life, it's just . . .

MIA. Look, it's fine, really, please, sit down, would you like a cup of tea?

GABRIEL. Oh, tea would be blinding.

MIA. Milk, sugar?

GABRIEL. Er . . . milk, no sugar, please.

MIA. OK, I won't be a minute.

She walks offstage, GABRIEL *remains sitting alone. He sighs, he seems stressed.*

GABRIEL (*to audience*). What do you do? You're given a job . . . you do your job . . .

He sighs.

. . . Things change though, that's the thing, and employers have to move with the times or they get left behind . . .

You can't just do things the way you always have and assume everyone is just going to keep up with you, 'cause they won't . . .

They won't.

You need to progress, evolve . . .

I know He hates that word, but it's true, you have to . . .

He sighs again.

I don't know . . .

Yes, fair enough, He started the whole thing but it doesn't mean He has a divine right to . . . well, it just doesn't work like that, people change, they move on and He of all people should know that . . .

There's no point being stubborn,

Yes, they *should* keep up, they *should* just stick to the ground rules but they don't . . .

He made them that way . . . in *His* image,

Sorry, I'm ranting, it's just . . .

It annoys me, you know? I'm the one that's out there, on the streets, on the front line. I see what things are like.

Things are different.

I don't get anywhere near the kind of respect or attention I used to . . .

Just look at today. I mean, it's not her fault, bless her, of course she's going to be a tad miffed, anyone would,

I would, but still, I am an angel for Heaven's sake, you'd have thought there'd be a little reverence, some awe maybe . . .

It's not *my* fault, I understand her stressing, but I don't make the . . .

I'm sorry, you don't want to hear this . . .

This is hardly reinstalling your faith in . . . faith, is it?

MIA *walks back in with two cups of tea and a packet of biscuits.*

Oh lovely, thank you very much.

MIA. You're welcome, thought I'd crack open the chocolate Hobnobs too, I can justify it now that I'm 'with child'.

GABRIEL. Indeed . . . eating for two, as they say.

They both smile, there is an awkward pause.

MIA. So . . . do you know how far gone I am?

GABRIEL. I'd say about six months?

MIA. Oh, six months? Goodness . . . three to go, I'd better start preparing. Cut back on the old . . . puff, puff, puff,

She mimes smoking a cigarette.

and the old . . . glug, glug, glug.

She mimes drinking a bottle of wine.

GABRIEL (*blankly*). Indeed, it may be an idea to cut back on the old . . .

He picks up the whip and 'cracks' it.

. . . as well.

MIA. Right . . .

GABRIEL. . . . just keeping up appearances, but . . .

MIA. Of course.

GABRIEL. Do you have anyone close who can help you?

MIA. Well, there's always Rebecca . . . she'll be a great help!

GABRIEL. Oh, fan of babies is she?

MIA. Rebecca, God no, she can't stand them, she has this dream where they look like her mum and dad and they shit and piss everywhere and she's running around and . . .

It doesn't matter . . .

Er, I'm sure my mother will help, she won't be very chuffed with the lack of partner, not a massive fan of the whole single mum thing but . . .

GABRIEL. Really? How does she feel about your . . . work then?

MIA. Oh, she doesn't know, she thinks I'm studying to be a marine biologist.

GABRIEL. I see . . .

Well, I'm sure she'll understand once you explain to her where the baby has come from . . .

MIA. Right, no, seriously, my mother will never go for the whole 'immaculate conception' thing. She'll think I've had sex with some married professor and I'm trying to cover for him.

GABRIEL. Professor?

MIA. From the university where I'm studying Coastal Zone and Marine Environment Studies . . .

No, it's always best to lie to your mother, that's the only way she'll ever believe you . . .

Besides, who, realistically, is going to believe that it was an immaculate conception? I'm not even a virgin . . . I'm a mistress!

GABRIEL. No, well, that's not our fault.

MIA (*insulted*). Oh yeah, oh well, that's fine then!

GABRIEL. I'm sorry, I didn't mean to . . . just, a hymen would help . . .

I could speak to your mother if you think it would make a difference?

MIA. I don't think that's a very good idea. She's got a weak heart and she's still angry with you lot about the death of Princess Diana.

GABRIEL. What? That wasn't our fault!

MIA. When you're all-seeing and all-knowing, everything's your fault.

GABRIEL. I see . . .

Beat.

MIA. Maybe it's best if people don't know anyway. If people know I'm carrying the child of God, well, the press'll get involved, people'll want to do tests, not to mention all the religious freaks, no offence, that'll be on my case . . . it's gonna make a lot of people nervous . . .

GABRIEL. Nervous? Why?

MIA. Armageddon, plague, pestilence, war, famine, you hardly publicised his return in a particularly favourable light.

GABRIEL. OK, so Revelations is a bit heavy, I didn't write it . . .

MIA. And that's just the believers, what about the people that think you don't even exist . . . ? I mean, isn't this whole thing all a bit too *Christian . . . ?* What about Islam, Judaism, Hinduism, Sikhism, Druzism, Gnosticism, Babism, Spiritualism, Taoism, Bahá'í . . .

GABRIEL. I . . .

MIA (*cutting him off*). Druidry, Paganism, not to mention the Orisha religions, the African religions, the Native American Indian religions . . .

GABRIEL. We . . .

MIA (*cutting him off*). Wicca, Kabbalah, the Scientologists, the Realists, to name but a few . . . don't they get a say in this? How are they going to feel about the return of Jesus . . . ?

GABRIEL. Bu . . .

MIA (*cutting him off*). And what about Gautama, Ganesha, the Buddha or Mohammed, peace be upon him, where are they in all this? Are they in there too? Curled up next to each other, waiting in line?

GABRIEL *stares at her dumbstruck.*

Sorry, I did RE. For my GSCEs, we considered it a bit of doss subject . . . like Drama . . .

Look, the point I'm trying to make is, if you exist, if *HE* exists then why hasn't he just come on down, said, 'Hi, I'm God . . . ' and explained the whole thing . . . He could do some big miracle like making the Eiffel Tower spin around or something – a good miracle – not setting alight to a bush for like three people to see, something big in front of everyone, prove it, confirm it, stop all the arguing and just . . . bang! This is it . . .

GABRIEL. Don't even talk to me about that. Believe me, I've had this conversation a thousand times, it's all about free will and . . . look, He's just a very stubborn deity.

MIA. So how do you expect us to know what to believe?

GABRIEL. Well . . . You believe in God, don't you?

MIA. Ah, but that's the thing . . . It's not a case of believing in *God*, is it? It's a case in believing in *Man*. God didn't write the Bible, Man did. It's Man's testimony, Man's version of events . . . It was Man who crucified Jesus in the first place! . . . And that was only because they thought he was being blasphemous . . . they thought they were doing the right thing by God! How do we know?

GABRIEL. OK, I understand it can all get a little confusing but . . .

MIA. . . . And while we're having this little Q and A, there's one more thing I never understood . . . If people are bad . . . they go to Hell, right? Where the Devil looks after them, instead of going to Heaven with you and God . . . But if they're bad and they're against God . . . then surely they'd be on the Devil's side, so why would he want to spend eternity torturing them? Surely he'd want to torture those who were good and reward those who were bad, like you do, but obviously the other way around . . .

GABRIEL. I . . . well . . . (*He is stumped, he fobs her off.*) Look, it's all in the book, is that not good enough for you?

MIA. There are a lot of things in a lot of books, you can't believe everything you read.

GABRIEL. You have read it though?

Beat.

MIA. Of course I've read it . . . most of it . . . If I'm honest Time Life has done a very good filmic adaptation.

GABRIEL. Really? I've not seen it.

MIA. Oh, it's great, it's got loads of famous people in it, Richard Harris, Christopher Lee, Gary Oldman, Ben Kingsley, Sean Bean, Diana Rigg, Dennis Hopper, Liz Hurley . . .

GABRIEL. Liz Hurley?

MIA. She plays Delilah.

GABRIEL. Right . . .

MIA. Michael Gambon, Oliver Reed, Leonard Nimoy . . .

GABRIEL. . . . is it any good?

MIA. Bit preachy but on the whole . . . hey, it's better than reading the thing!

GABRIEL. . . . Am I in it? Who plays me?

MIA. Er, I'm not sure actually, I've got it boxed up somewhere, we could take a look . . .

GABRIEL. Well, if it's not too much trouble, just out of curiosity . . .

MIA. No trouble at all. I think it's in the loft though, so you'll have to go up and get it.

GABRIEL. Not a problem, I'm good with heights.

They exit the room, upstage left. Moments later, the CHORUS *enter upstage right, minus the actor who plays* GABRIEL.

The dramatic chorus music plays.

CHORUS.
And so the revelation was unveiled
The babe inside her would a King be hailed . . .

Suddenly the actor playing GABRIEL *rushes on to join the* CHORUS. *He has his mask on but is still wearing his* GABRIEL *costume. The* CHORUS *turn to look at him, maintaining the stylised action of their choral movement. They restart.*

And so the revelation was unveiled
The babe inside her would a King be hailed
But resolved our story still is not
For lurks another factor she forgot.
A Fallen Angel known by many names
Will soon turn up to lay another claim
Not to mention two more mortal men
Who think the baby may belong to them,
And the dear friend who's betrayed our muse
Will soon appear to further things confuse.

But all this you shall very soon be told
So now the story we shall let unfold.

The CHORUS *exit upstage right,* MIA *re-enters upstage left.*

MIA (*shouting off*). I'm sure it's on one of those shelves, just keep looking . . .

She closes the door and takes a deep breath, a beat, to try and take in everything she's just found out. She looks to the audience and addresses them.

Well, fuck me sideways . . . me . . . the Mother of God . . .

Well, that's a turn-up for the books . . .

So what now?

How am I supposed to bring up a Messiah on my own?

It'll be like some messy divorce . . . an absentee father, always around in 'spirit' but never in person, never there to do the hard stuff, the arguments and the punishment, which means Mummy gets labelled as the bad guy, never able to live up to the father's perfect, God-like image and so the child is always sulking, saying he wants to go and live with his dad because 'Daddy lets me wear my sandals indoors and Daddy lets me play with lepers . . . '

Oh God, he'll be a nightmare . . . Little boys are a fucking curse at the best of times, even when they're not divine.

How are you supposed to discipline the Son of God?

How do you tell the Son of God that if he doesn't do his homework he'll amount to nothing . . . ?

Hey, maybe it'll be a girl . . . ? (*Sarcastically.*) Yeah, right.

There is a knock at the door and she goes to answer it. It's MICHAEL, *he bursts in.*

MICHAEL. I've just spoken to Rebecca, she told me . . .

FUCK YOU'RE PREGNANT, IT'S TRUE, LOOK AT YOU, YOU'RE FUCKING MASSIVE!

MIA (*sarcastic*). Michael, how lovely to see you, please do come in.

MICHAEL. I don't believe this, how did this happen?

I told you to be careful,

I asked you every time if it was OK,

If you were on the pill,

You promised me . . .

Oh God, I see it,

That's what this is . . . THIS IS ENTRAPMENT,

You're trying to get me back, you thought a baby would . . .

OH YEAH, OH WELL, I'M ON TO YOU, MISSY.

MIA. Michael, we broke up well over nine months ago . . .

MICHAEL. Don't give me that, I know that . . . I oh . . .

OH . . .

It can't be mine . . . because we broke up over nine months ago . . . so we haven't had sex for over nine months . . . which is how long a baby takes . . . which means it isn't mine . . .

Ha, you've got nothing . . . it can't be mine . . .

I'm fine, I'M FINE!

Beat.

Well, you didn't waste any time, did you? Fucking hell, I'm gone five minutes and you're pregnant . . . that's just fucking . . . careless . . .

MIA. Bloody hell, Michael, you're such an idiot.

MICHAEL. What? WHAT!? You're the . . .

GABRIEL *re-enters upstage left.*

MIA. A pig, Michael, that's the word for you, a pig.

MICHAEL. Aaargh, you are the living end . . .

GABRIEL. It's no good, I looked through the cast list on the back of all of them but I couldn't see my name anywhere . . .

MICHAEL. Who the fuck's this?

MIA. This is Gabriel.

MICHAEL. Oh Gabriel, of course, it's *Gabriel*, why didn't you say so. Hello Gabriel, how are you . . . ?

WHO THE FUCK IS GABRIEL?

GABRIEL. I . . .

MIA. It's his baby . . .

GABRIEL. Well, no, it's not actually mine . . .

MICHAEL. You are unbelievable, UNBELIEVABLE . . .

You just . . . the first thing that comes along . . .

Let's have a fucking baby . . . It's sad,

That's what it is . . .

You know what? It's the fucking baby I feel sorry for.

MIA. Oh, don't be such a prick.

GABRIEL. As I say, not technically my baby . . .

MICHAEL. Oh right, of course it's not, you probably don't even know who the father is, Gabriel here is just the latest poor sap you've found to drag in and take on the responsibility. Some married man with a lot of money, what, are you blackmailing him or something? Sending dirty pictures to his wife?

MIA. Oh Michael, for fuck's sake . . . What if I am? Why would you care? YOU LEFT ME . . .

MICHAEL. It was mutual!

MIA. Mutual!

They start shouting over the top of each other.

You are such a prick! You can't even accept responsibility for . . .

MICHAEL. . . . We were both changing but we weren't allowing each other to move on, everything else in our lives was progressing but we were forcing each other to stay as the people we KNEW, which weren't the people that we WERE any more . . .

MIA. THAT IS BOLLOCKS!

MICHAEL. DON'T . . . look . . . this isn't about that . . .

MIA. Well, what is this about . . . ?

MICHAEL. YOUR BABY!

MIA. Well, what the hell has MY baby go to do with YOU?

MICHAEL. I . . .

Well . . .

FINE!

GABRIEL. Look, I could go and come back if . . .

MIA. No, Gabriel, you stay.

MICHAEL. Yes, Gabriel, you stay, sit down, put your feet up. Hey, make another baby while you're here, don't mind me.

MIA. Michael, Gabriel is an angel.

GABRIEL. *Arch*angel.

MIA. *Arch*angel, and he is here to tell me that my conception was immaculate.

MICHAEL *stares at her.*

. . . It's the second coming.

MICHAEL *stares at her.*

. . . I'm carrying God's baby.

MICHAEL *stares at her. Beat.*

He looks at GABRIEL, *then back to* MIA.

Silence.

MICHAEL. Could I have a word with you a second?

He looks at MIA, *she looks back, he ushers her to the front of the stage, he looks back to* GABRIEL *who smiles politely.*

(*Whispering.*) What in the blue hell are you trying to pull here?

MIA. I'm not trying to pull anything, he just turned up and told me that I'm carrying God's baby.

MICHAEL. What, and you believed him?

MIA. Well, no, not really, not at first. But . . .

MICHAEL. Christ, your ego astounds me! Anyone else would laugh him out of the fucking country but you . . . 'Well, I suppose I would be quite a good choice, and God obviously knows what he's doing . . . '

You're meant to be a fucking atheist!

MIA. Hey look, he had this scroll . . .

MICHAEL. Oh, he had a scroll? Well, if he had a scroll, he must be an angel . . .

Why would angels have scrolls for fuck's sake?! Pirates have scrolls, other mythical beings from the Middle Ages have scrolls, you make scrolls at school, by dipping bits of paper in tea. I made several fairly convincing ones, I even got my dad to help me put a wax stamp on them using one of my mother's Christmas candles and a pound coin but that does not make me a herald of God!

MIA. Michael, I taught you sarcasm and now you're just using it against me.

MICHAEL. Has he asked you for any money?

MIA. No! Look, Michael, it has to be true . . . what other explanation is there?

MICHAEL. For fuck's sake, I thought you'd know the mechanics of it by now. The man takes his special wand and puts it into the lady's . . .

MIA. Michael, I haven't had sex since you!

MICHAEL. I . . . oh . . . well . . .

Beat.

Really?

Beat.

But it's been like a year?

MIA. Yes, Michael.

MICHAEL. . . . No one?

MIA. No, Michael.

MICHAEL. . . . Not even a . . . ?

MIA. No, Michael.

MICHAEL. A little . . . ?

MIA. No, Michael.

MICHAEL. Not on the . . .

MIA. No, Michael.

MICHAEL. With a . . .

MIA. No, Michael.

MICHAEL. Up the . . .

MIA. NO, MICHAEL!

Beat.

MICHAEL. Fucking hell! But . . . a year?

MIA. OK, I think we've established this.

Beat.

MICHAEL (*nodding knowingly*). You're still in love with me.

She slaps him on the chest dismissively.

OK . . . But if you haven't had sex for . . . then how are you pregnant?

MIA. Exactly!

MICHAEL *stares at her, then at* GABRIEL.

MICHAEL. . . . Let me see this scroll.

They both shuffle over to GABRIEL *sheepishly,* MICHAEL *mumbles to* GABRIEL *under his breath, embarrassed.*

Could we see your scroll, please?

GABRIEL *sighs and hands him the scroll.* MICHAEL *and* MIA *then shuffle off again to inspect it.* MICHAEL *reads it closely.*

Well, it's a good scroll, I'll give him that.

MIA. What other explanation can there be?

GABRIEL. Look er . . .

MICHAEL. . . . Michael.

GABRIEL. Michael, I know it can be a little overwhelming but God's love can . . .

MICHAEL (*cutting him off*). Maybe he's just trying to convert you . . . maybe this is a new technique they're using to tackle dwindling church attendance numbers.

MIA (*looking down at her large bump*). It's a bit extreme, don't you think?

GABRIEL. Look, Michael, I'm not here to trick anyone, or convert anyone, or save anyone, I'm a messenger, that's all . . .

GABRIEL *delivers the next speech as if rehearsed, with the lights slowly fading to a spot on him, and 'Jerusalem' (or another piece of stirring religious music) underscoring his speech. As the music builds, so does* GABRIEL's *delivery. Throughout,* MIA *and* MICHAEL *look increasingly confused at what is happening. At the end of the speech, the music abruptly cuts and the lights snap back to normal.*

'She has found favour with God, she is with child and will give birth to a son, and she is to give Him the name Jesus. He will be great and will be called the Son of the Most High. The Lord God will give Him the throne of his father

David, and He will reign over the house of Jacob forever;
His kingdom will never end.'

MICHAEL *and* MIA *stare at* GABRIEL. *There is a long pause.*

MIA. Well, I'm going to make some more tea . . . Gabriel?

GABRIEL. Oh yes please.

MICHAEL. I'll have . . .

MIA. Not you, go home.

MIA *exits upstage left leaving* MICHAEL *and* GABRIEL
alone. There is a long awkward pause.

MICHAEL *wanders over to* GABRIEL *and hands him the
scroll. He mumbles under his breath.*

MICHAEL. Here's your scroll.

GABRIEL. Thank you.

MICHAEL. It's a good scroll.

GABRIEL. Yes.

MICHAEL. I made one once, wasn't as good.

GABRIEL. Oh . . . better luck next time.

There is another long pause, MICHAEL *thinks desperately
of a way to break the silence.*

MICHAEL. So, Gabriel . . . how long have you been an angel?

GABRIEL. Oh, a good few thousand years.

MICHAEL. Right . . . enjoy it?

GABRIEL. Yes, most of the time. You know, long hours, lot of
travelling but . . .

MICHAEL. Right . . . Do you have . . . ?

GABRIEL. Wings? No, afraid not.

MICHAEL. I was going to say a harp but . . .

GABRIEL. That's cherubs.

MICHAEL. Right . . .

Beat.

. . . Remind me of the difference again?

GABRIEL. Cherubs are babies.

MICHAEL. Right, babies, of course.

Beat.

So . . . how am I doing?

GABRIEL. Excuse me?

MICHAEL. You know, with him upstairs . . . am I on his list of good little boys and girls, or bad ones?

GABRIEL. I think you're confusing him with Father Christmas.

MICHAEL. Right, yes . . . I didn't mean, not the list obviously, I just meant, you know . . . am I doing OK?

GABRIEL. I'm afraid I'm not at liberty to divulge that sort of information.

MICHAEL. Right . . . right, but you'd give me a heads-up if I was heading, you know, in the wrong direction sort of thing?

GABRIEL. I'm afraid it's not my place, I'd be compromising your free will.

MICHAEL. Of course, of course . . . wouldn't want that . . . But you know, you wouldn't just let me . . .

GABRIEL. I think I'll just go and make sure she's alright with the tea.

MICHAEL. Right . . .

GABRIEL *exits upstage left,* MICHAEL *is alone. To audience:*

. . . This is so typical of her.

She always has to be different, she can't do things the normal way, no . . . she makes a lasagne; she can't just buy a jar of white Ragu, no, she has to make the white sauce herself.

She decorates the bedroom; she can't just use the four pots of Magnolia her dad had left over from their lounge, no, she wants Quince which is two shades lighter and four times more expensive.

She has a baby; she can't just have any baby, no, it has to be 'God's' baby . . .

I should have known she'd pull something like this.

If I didn't know better I'd say she was trying to get me back.

The Mother of God, Christ Almighty! I bet she's *absolutely loving* that. She's always acted 'holier than thou' and now she really is . . .

I've got to say she strikes me as an odd choice . . . don't get me wrong, I'm sure she'll be very good, but if he's looking for a little woman to stay indoors and keep her mouth shut then he's in for a bit of a shock.

It's quite a scary thought really; I mean, who's the one person with more power than God . . . his mother! God help . . . himself.

Well, I suppose I should look on the bright side . . .

At least it's not *mine* . . .

Which is a good thing; I mean, I don't want a kid, I'm not ready to settle down yet and I certainly wouldn't want *her* kid.

Me and her are over, finished. What we had is gone . . .

It's not like I carry any sort of torch for her or anything ridiculous like that!

It's finished, thanks but no thanks, I'm done!

Yes, I care about her of course but . . .

Beat.

OK so she's the only woman I've ever truly been in love with . . . but that's so far, you know?

I broke up with her and I'm glad.

It was absolutely the right decision, *we were both changing but we were forcing each other to stay as* . . . well, it was the right thing to do and like the saying goes, the grass is always greener on the other side of the fence and it really is. I mean, my grass at the moment is really, really green, it's like . . . a lizard . . . it's so green it's practically brown . . .

GABRIEL *and* MIA *re-enter upstage left, carrying teas.*

MIA (*mid-conversation*). . . . So it's not like Scientology where you're not allowed any drugs?

GABRIEL. Oh no, you can have as many drugs as you want . . .

MIA *notices* MICHAEL.

MIA. . . . Are you still here?

MICHAEL. Of course I'm still here.

MIA. Why?

MICHAEL. Well, we . . . I mean, I can't just leave you here with some random man.

MIA. Michael, he's an angel.

MICHAEL. Yes, well . . . so was David Boreanaz . . . and he was also a vampire!

MIA. What?

MICHAEL. From *Buffy*?

MIA. Yes, I know who David Boreanaz is . . . And he wasn't an angel, he was just called Angel . . . and it was a fictional television series!

MICHAEL. Right, well, I'm just trying to illustrate . . .

MIA. Go home, Michael.

MICHAEL. But what if . . . ?

MIA. HOME!

MICHAEL. Fine, I'll leave you with weirdy beardy, I hope you're very happy, get a cloud together for all I care, I try and be a gentleman and what do I get but . . .

MIA. GOODBYE MICHAEL!

MICHAEL. . . . FINE!

> MICHAEL *goes to the door and opens it. There is a man,* LUCIFER, *standing there.*

. . . Who the fuck are you?

LUCIFER. I'm Lucifer, I'm here for my baby.

MICHAEL. Of course, of course you are, come in, join the queue . . .

> LUCIFER *steps past a bewildered* MICHAEL, *and moves towards* MIA, *he doesn't notice* GABRIEL.

LUCIFER. . . . and this must be the mother to be, enchanté, may I say you look fantastic. If I'm honest with you, I think the term 'glowing' is tossed around far too loosely when talking about pregnant women but you really do seem to be emitting some kind of wonderful . . . aura, you're radiant, you look fabulous!

GABRIEL. Alright, alright, enough, bravo, you're too late . . .

LUCIFER. Oh God, what are you doing here?

GABRIEL. This one's one of ours.

LUCIFER. No, sorry, no way, G, this baby's mine.

GABRIEL. I'm sorry, Luci . . .

LUCIFER. Don't push me, Gabriel . . .

GABRIEL. Lucifer . . .

LUCIFER. Don't you . . .

GABRIEL. It's not . . .

LUCIFER. No.

GABRIEL. You . . .

LUCIFER. No, you can shove it up your big fat fucking angel anus, this is my fucking baby!

GABRIEL. Do you have to use such vile language? There are ladies present.

LUCIFER. What? Oh, excuse me, Gabriel, does my fucking language fucking upset you, you mother-fucking, cock-sucking, pig-fucker?

GABRIEL. No, Lucifer, your juvenile potty mouth doesn't upset me, it embarrasses me . . .

The fact that the alleged ruler of all evil isn't eloquent enough to string together a suitable sentence without having to resort to the repeated use of expletives makes me feel embarrassed . . . (*Beat.*) for you!

LUCIFER *slowly raises his middle finger at* GABRIEL.

MIA (*cutting them off*). Hello . . . ? Lady with a baby?

Forgive me for asking . . . who are you?

MICHAEL. Beautiful, don't even know the father's name!

GABRIEL. He's not the father.

LUCIFER. Yes I am.

GABRIEL. No you're not.

LUCIFER. I think you'll find I am . . .

GABRIEL. He's not.

LUCIFER. Er, I think you'll find I am.

GABRIEL. Er, I think *you'll* find . . .

MIA. BOYS! Please . . .

Beat. A mobile phone rings. (*Note: a novelty ringtone may be used for added comic effect.*)

MICHAEL. Sorry . . . that's me, I'll just . . .

He walks out the door upstage right with his phone.

MIA. You . . . (*To* LUCIFER.) Speak!

LUCIFER. Thank you.

He prepares himself for his big speech.

I am Lucifer, the Prince of Darkness. Around six months ago there was a momentous night, a night that would change the fate of all mankind, a night when the heavens kissed and the sun blinked and the Fallen Angel would walk the earth once more . . .

GABRIEL. Blah blaah blah blaah . . .

LUCIFER. Gabriel, come on, be fair, this is my turn. She said I could speak.

MIA *glares at him.* GABRIEL *huffs angrily, makes a zip gesture across his mouth, folds his arms and sulks.* MIA *nods supportively at* LUCIFER *to continue.*

. . . On this night I would be allowed to take the body of another mortal for one solitary hour, in that hour I would find my bride and sow my seed and so my spawn would . . .

MICHAEL *walks noisily back in through the door upstage right.* LUCIFER *trails off frustrated by this second interruption, everyone stares at* MICHAEL.

MICHAEL. Sorry, work, there's this thing . . .

LUCIFER *sighs, defeated.*

LUCIFER. . . . Look, I took a body, had sex with you and now you've got my baby.

MICHAEL. Nice . . . romantic.

MIA. Michael, what are you even doing here?

MICHAEL. I . . . FINE!

GABRIEL. Actually, Lucifer, I think you'll find, if you ask her, that she hasn't had sex with anyone since him and that was well over nine months ago.

MICHAEL. *Well over.*

MIA. Man's got a point.

LUCIFER. Actually, Gabrielle, I think you'll find she has had sex, I should know, I was there . . .

GABRIEL. Actually, Lucifer, I think you'll find . . .

LUCIFER. Actually, Gabriel, you're a dick!

MIA (*cutting them off*). BOYS!

MICHAEL*'s mobile goes again.*

MICHAEL. Sorry . . . I'll . . .

Everyone stares at him, he looks uncomfortable.

Sorry, I'll just . . .

He answer it sheepishly.

Hello . . . yes . . . yep . . .

He looks at everyone nervously.

. . . yeah . . . hang on . . .

He moves downstage right to try and get some privacy and continues his conversation in a forced whisper, obviously keen not to be heard. Throughout the phone call, GABRIEL, LUCIFER and MIA try to eavesdrop on the conversation, slowly and subtly they edge their way across the stage closer to MICHAEL until they are practically on top of him. (Note: you may wish to play the high-pitched squeak of a voice as if at the other end of the phone line to coincide with MICHAEL's conversation.)

. . . Look, I can't talk, yes, I'm still here . . .

No, I told you, it's not mine . . .

I know it's not mine because I haven't had sex with her in nine months . . .

Which is how long a baby takes . . .

Yes, I'm sure . . .

Look, I told you this, *she's* told you this . . .

Why would I lie . . . ?

Why would she lie?

Well, that's just ridiculous . . .

NO . . . !

Look, there are two men here, both claiming to be the
father . . .

Yes, two . . .

Well, *I* don't know why she hasn't told you about them –
ask her . . .

No, I will not put her on . . .

Look, this is hardly the best time to . . .

No . . . I . . . well, that's . . . don't . . . you . . . I . . . but . . .
NO . . . DON'T . . .

DON'T YOU . . . NO . . . Just . . .

HELLO . . . ?

HELLO?

MICHAEL *turns and realises everyone is standing right
next to him.* MIA, GABRIEL *and* LUCIFER *pretend to be
engaged in some other conversation so as not to give away
the fact they have been blatantly eavesdropping.*

Sorry . . . work, there's this thing . . .

There is an awkward silence.

MIA. Anything you wanna share?

MICHAEL. No, no it's fine . . . all . . . everything's . . . yeah . . .

There is another awkward silence.

LUCIFER. Shall I . . . ?

They all nod and encourage LUCIFER *to carry on,
welcoming the distraction from such an awkward moment.*

MIA. Yes, sorry, Lucifer, you go on . . .

LUCIFER. Right well, as I was saying, I took a body, I had sex
with you, hence the baby . . .

MIA. But Lucifer . . . I haven't had sex for nearly a year . . .

LUCIFER (*smugly*). Oh no? The words GOOD . . . MAN don't ring any bells?

He pulls a Dictaphone from his pocket and presses play – it plays a tacky 'DUN DUN DAH!' sound.

MIA (*staring at him confused – long beat*). . . . No.

LUCIFER. Excuse me.

He turns away sheepishly, we hear him rewind his Dictaphone.

GOOD MAN?!

He presses his Dictaphone again, the same 'DUN DUN DAH!' plays.

MIA (*staring at him, still confused. Beat*). . . . No, nothing?

LUCIFER *sighs, defeated again.*

LUCIFER. Goodman?

MIA *stares at him, trying to figure it out – long beat – a look of absolute horror edges across her face.*

MIA. OH MY GOD . . . GARY GOODMAN!

Blackout.

In the blackout we hear the 'DUN DUN DAH!' play again.

End of Act One.

ACT TWO

The CHORUS *stand on stage. The actors playing* GABRIEL,
MICHAEL *and* LUCIFER *all wear their character costumes
with their chorus masks. The actress playing* REBECCA,
however, is still in black. The dramatic chorus music plays.

CHORUS.
Previously upon this very stage
We spoke of birth foretold on holy page
We offer to you now a brief recap
For those of you whose memories are crap.
Our lead, Mia by name, Mistress by trade
Has fallen pregnant without getting laid.
Two angels both are claiming fatherhood
One part of all that's bad, the other good.
There's also Michael, Mia's moody ex
Who's stunned it's been a year since she's had sex
And now the bombshell's broke of an old flame,
Who turns out less than good despite his name.
So now we're up to speed, well what the heck!
Let's kick off Act Two in the discotheque.

*The serious chorus music suddenly transforms into disco
music.*

The CHORUS *move to reveal a bar. They remove their
masks and put them on the hatstand, suddenly acting as if
they are in a disco. The actor playing* LUCIFER *becomes
the barman, whilst the actors playing* MICHAEL *and*
GABRIEL *become punters at the bar. The actor playing*
REBECCA *exits the stage and* MIA *enters. She goes up to
the bar and orders a glass of wine.*

Moments later, GARY GOODMAN *bursts through the
door. He's a dick, slimy, irritating, lecherous, he nods at the
guys, nodding his head to the music. It is clear he has
co-ordination issues. When he spies* MIA, *his eyes light up.*

(Note: if at all possible have the actor playing GARY
GOODMAN *come in through the audience. It is important
to establish the character of* GARY *before the dialogue
starts.)*

GARY. OH MY GOD, it's YOU!

MIA. Sorry, do I know you?

GARY. Er yes . . . it's me, Gary, the Big G . . . the Good
Man . . . We had CDT together with Mr Phillips, I cut my
finger off and we had to use your scarf as a tourniquet?

MIA. Oh my God, oh my God, yes, Gary Goodman. God, how
are you?

GARY. I'm good, I'm really good actually, just been promoted,
yeah, I'm into property, yeah. Head of lettings, not bad
considering I'm the youngest in my office . . .

MIA. Wow . . .

GARY. Yeah . . . well, you put the work in, it pays dividends,
you know . . . I earned it . . . I'm young . . . fresh . . . I've
still got the hunger, that's what makes me special . . . I work
hard . . . still play hard though . . . hard as ice . . .

MIA. Rrright . . .

GARY. Oh yes, work out four times a week too, so I'm
literally hard as well . . . and I drive a TT.

He pulls out his wallet and shows her a picture of his car.

MIA. Nice.

GARY. Yeah, it is, I call him Mr T . . . T.

I like Audis, you know, well-made cars, looks good but it's
got the muscle to back it up, if you know what I mean,
which is something I like to think I strive for in life . . .
Look, I'll buy you a drink . . .

MIA. Really, I'm . . .

GARY. Wine, yeah?

He takes her wine glass and drinks it.

That's shit . . .

I'll pick you something.

Barman . . . ?

Barman . . . ?

Barman . . . ?

The BARMAN *disappears behind the bar.*

MIA (*turning to the audience*). Oh my God, Gary Goodman,
I used to go to school with him . . . He was a DICK!

GARY. Barman!

MIA. He was one of those dicks that didn't know he was a
dick and laughed when people took the piss out of him . . .
a friendly dick, as if he was allowing you to take the piss
out of him 'cause he knew it was his only way into the
conversation . . .

Dick!

GARY. Barman!

MIA. He covered all his schoolbooks with wrapping paper and
wore waistcoats to school discos.

He always used to fancy me . . .

I remember for three years in a row he got me Valentine
cards. He used to sign them with question marks but I knew
they'd come from him because he used to give them to
Rebecca to give to me. I'm not sure how he thought she
wouldn't tell me, or maybe he thought she would tell me
and then I'd declare my mutual undying love for him . . .

Which I wouldn't have done because he was a dick . . .

GARY. BARMAN!!

MIA. He could never drink Coke because it made him hyper
and he'd get these weird red marks on his face and chest . . .

I remember once at Adrian Morgan's birthday party when
Duncan Carson made him drink a pint of Coke and he went
crazy, just buzzing and running around, he started squeaking

in a really high-pitched voice then passed out and pissed himself,

Adrian's mum had to call an ambulance, it was quite scary at the time . . .

I remember the following Monday at school he told us that the doctor had said he nearly died . . .

He still had massive red marks on his neck that were shaped like seahorses . . . crazy.

Back to the scene.

GARY. BARMAN . . .

The BARMAN *suddenly pops up from behind the bar.*

BAR . . . Hi, cool, yes, er, I'll have a bottle of your finest champagne, sir.

BARMAN. We don't do champagne . . . we've got some cava, I think . . .

GARY. Perfect, what year?

BARMAN. I don't know, last year? It's not that old.

GARY. I'm sure it'll be fine . . . two glasses, and get yourself something.

BARMAN. I don't drink, I'm a recovering alcoholic . . .

GARY. Fine, just the cava then, and the glasses, thanks . . .

The BARMAN *disappears behind the bar.*

Yeah . . . so . . . enough about me . . . boring . . . how are you?

The BARMAN *pops up from behind the bar.*

BARMAN. The cava's this year, do you still want it?

GARY. Yes . . . please . . . fine, thank you . . .

Suddenly GARY*'s phone starts to ring, he answers it.*

Again a novelty ringtone can be used – perhaps one GARY *has recorded for himself.*

Hello . . . Casanova's phone . . . No no, it's Gary . . . No,
Gary? Gary Goodman, this is Gary Goodman's phone?
Sorry mate, I'm in a club, it's banging! Yeah, Gary
Goodman . . . Gary Goodman?

He looks to MIA.

Sorry, babe, five minutes, don't go anywhere, yeah?

Back to the phone.

No Gary GOODMAN, GARY GOODMAN, it's GARY
GOODMAN . . .

GARY GOODMAN . . .

GARY GOODMAN . . .

GARY *exits upstage right, still on the phone, still shouting
'Gary Goodman' as if as an echo. The image of the bar then
disintegrates, the lights come up and the disco music comes
to an end.*

Suddenly we are back in MIA*'s flat, with everyone in the
same positions as at the end of Act One.*

MIA*'s 'Gary Goodman' should come straight in after*
GARY*'s 'Gary Goodman', as if a continuation of the same
thought.*

MIA. Gary Goodman!

Fuck . . . no . . . no no no, I did not have sex with Gary
Goodman . . .

MICHAEL. Gary Goodman, oh my God!

MIA. But it wasn't Gary Goodman . . . it was you . . . right?

LUCIFER. No, *that* wasn't me, I didn't turn up 'til much later
in the evening.

MICHAEL. Gary Goodman?

GABRIEL. Who's Gary Goodman?

MICHAEL. He pissed himself at Adrian Morgan's birthday
party 'cause he drunk too much Coke.

GABRIEL. Oh . . . who's Adrian Morgan?

MIA. Hang on, you had one night on Earth to get laid, you could pick any *body* you wanted and you picked Gary Goodman's?

LUCIFER. What's wrong with Gary Goodman?

MICHAEL. HELLO?

LUCIFER. It worked, didn't it?

MIA. No, you must have drugged me or something, used some black magic, or your devil powers to seduce me.

LUCIFER. Love, by the time I turned up, there wasn't a lot of seducing needed, if you know what I mean . . . you were all over me.

MIA. OH GOD, NO! Please God, no, don't let this be true.

LUCIFER. . . . I wouldn't necessarily have picked you but you didn't leave me with a lot of choice.

MIA. God, no, please say that you're lying, please . . .

LUCIFER. I don't know how much champagne you'd drunk but it was all I could do to get you back to your flat.

MIA. OH GOD, NO NO NO, it wasn't even champagne, it was cava! OH GOD!

GABRIEL. I don't suppose you could change your use of curse words?

MIA. Fuck off.

GABRIEL. Thank you.

MICHAEL. Gary Goodman? You slept with Gary Goodman?

LUCIFER. Well, technically she slept with me . . .

MIA. Oh no, no no no, what was I doing?

MICHAEL. Unbelievable.

MIA. I want to die . . .

She puts her head in her hands.

LUCIFER. What is so wrong with Gary Goodman?

There is a knock at the door, everything stops.

MICHAEL. Shit!

It knocks again. GABRIEL *gets up and moves to the door.*

No, don't open it . . . it's probably a wrong . . . number.

Everyone stares at MICHAEL. *Another knock, more violently,* GABRIEL *opens it.* REBECCA *walks in, she doesn't look happy.* MICHAEL *cringes.*

REBECCA (*all gabbled at an incredible rate*). Hi . . . Look, there's something I have to say. I probably should have told you earlier, but I didn't know if it was going anywhere but now I think it is, or thought it was, but now you're pregnant, so I probably shouldn't tell you anyway 'cause stress is bad for the baby, not that you're keeping it, right? God, you're huge, are those my boots . . . ?

Look . . . Michael and I are together . . .

We're a couple, I'm sorry I didn't tell you, I didn't plan it, I was out and saw Michael and said hello and we got talking and it came out that he'd always quite fancied me but couldn't do anything about it obviously 'cause we were best mates and I said I quite fancied him too, which was why I was sometimes a bit of a bitch towards him because I think subconsciously I fancied him and I always used to talk to Ed about him, and that's why Ed never wanted to come out with us in a foursome because he thought I fancied Michael which I didn't, or didn't think I did, but turns out I did, because I fancy him now, anyway, we weren't going to do anything because you two had just broken up and I knew how pissed off you'd be but then we said, well, maybe we should just have a kiss, while we're both single then, just to get it out of our systems, so we had a kiss, and then the kiss carried on, and things and things and we ended up having sex, which I'm not proud of but it was good, but it was bad because the condom broke and I had to get the morning-after pill, which was fucking awful and I was terrified 'cause I thought I was gonna have a baby, and you know how much I fucking hate babies 'cause of that dream I have with all the babies that have my mum and dad's faces who shit and piss and cry and I can't stop them! And also the pill made me feel really ill, and that was the day we were supposed to go to Bluewater to try and find some shoes to go with that brown skirt you got from Hennes and I said I couldn't come 'cause I was sick and you were pissed off and I wanted to tell you but I couldn't and I felt really guilty, and I cried, and then I called Michael and told him and he was really good about it and made me feel better, and we had decided we weren't gonna see each other again, but I was crying on the phone so he came over and then he ended up staying the night again, but we didn't have sex, we just cuddled and then it went from there.

But now you tell me that you're pregnant and you say that you haven't had sex with anyone since Michael, which means he must be the father but you don't want to tell me because I made such a fuss about what a fucker he was when he dumped you. Which means you're lying to me and he's lying to me, and I'm lying to you, and you're fucking him and I'm fucking him and he's fucking you . . . and me . . . and I'm going to lose my best friend and my boyfriend, not that I call him my boyfriend but technically he is, and I'll be helpless and hopeless and friendless and loveless and die old and alone with thread veins and bladder weakness and a houseful of cats . . .

There is silence. Everyone is trying to take in what has just happened.

MIA. . . . You . . . ? You two? YOU TWO? I don't believe it, you two?

To MICHAEL.

You absolute fucker, how could you? 'I need space, I'm changing, I want to be on my own . . . '

MICHAEL. I did . . .

MIA. My best friend? You always said you thought she was a whiney cow.

REBECCA. Excuse me?

MIA. You said she was more irritating than eczema and now you're fucking her? You utter scumbag, you utter shit-crawling, sewer-dredging, pus-sucking, piss-drinking, dog-fucking, lying, cheating, dickless little scumbag . . . (*To* REBECCA.) My best friend, how could you? What are you? How do . . . And you?

REBECCA. I know, I'm sorry, I hate myself.

MIA. All that time, you lying, disgusting, two-faced bitchy little whorebag . . . all that time.

REBECCA. I know, I'm sorry, I didn't mean it, I couldn't help it . . .

I love him!

MICHAEL. Whoahhh!

MIA. Love him? LOVE HIM? Why? He's an anus!

REBECCA. You can't talk, you're fucking him!

MIA. I most certainly am not.

REBECCA. Look, you don't have to lie to me, I know what's going on, I know you're sleeping with him.

MIA. What if I was? He's MY boyfriend.

MICHAEL. *Ex*-boyfriend.

MIA. Yes, *ex*-boyfriend, thank fuck, because you're A PRICK! He's a prick, why would you sleep with him?

REBECCA. Why are *you* sleeping with him?

MIA. I'M NOT!

MICHAEL. SEE!

REBECCA. BUT YOU'RE PREGNANT!

MIA. SO?

REBECCA. Then who's the father?

MICHAEL. GARY GOODMAN!

REBECCA. GARY GOODMAN? WHAT!?

Beat.

Oh my God, you had sex with Gary Goodman?

MIA. NO, I had sex with HIM. (*Pointing to* LUCIFER.)

LUCIFER. I'm sorry, I just don't see what is so bad about Gary Goodman?

REBECCA. You had sex with Gary Goodman and you didn't tell me?

MIA. You had sex with my BOYFRIEND and didn't tell me.

MICHAEL. EX-boyfriend.

MIA. YES, EX-boyfriend and I thank my fucking lucky stars because you are the king of all DICKS!

REBECCA. When?

GABRIEL. Six months ago.

REBECCA. Gary Goodman? What was he, a client?

MIA. Forget about Gary Goodman, Gary Goodman is not the issue here, the issue here is you two.

LUCIFER. A client?

GABRIEL. She's a prostitute.

LUCIFER. She's a prostitute and she hasn't had sex for nine months?

MIA. I'm not a prostitute. I'm a mistress, it's very different.

Beat.

Everyone takes a deep breath before 'Round Two' starts up.

LUCIFER. You say potato and I say potato.

GABRIEL. I think you'll find it's pot-*ah*-to.

LUCIFER (*over the top of each other*). Why do you always have to pick me up on everything?

MIA (*over the top of each other*). Look, what the fuck do potatoes have to do with . . .

MICHAEL (*over the top of each other*). Don't have a go at
him . . .

MIA, MICHAEL, GABRIEL *and* LUCIFER *all descend
into an argument, as this happens their dialogue fades out
and a voice-over of* REBECCA *fades up. As her voice-over
plays,* REBECCA *is standing separately from the rest of the
cast reacting as if we are hearing her thoughts. The others
continue to argue in silence in the background.*

REBECCA (*voice-over*). Typical, I end up looking like the real
bitch again.

Bear in mind we're telling *her* story at the moment, I mean,
think about *my* story for a second.

It's not easy being her best friend, you know. Look at her,
she's intelligent, attractive, great set of tits . . .

All these dry sarcastic one-liners might seem funny but
when you've been best friends with it for ten years, they
start to grate . . .

I remember what she said to me when my boob popped out
at our Year 10 roller disco?

'Don't worry, there wasn't much of it to see anyway.'

I've worn chicken fillets ever since.

My point is I really care about Michael. I mean, really
underneath it all, he's a lovely, genuine, caring guy . . .

As she says this, we see MICHAEL *in the background,
silently screaming at the others.*

. . . they just rub each other up the wrong way, I mean, he
would never . . . we've always . . .

She thinks for a second, remembering something.

. . . hang on . . .

*Lights suddenly come up, breaking the thought process, she
is suddenly back in the room with the others.*

REBECCA (*out loud, as a continuation of the same thought*).
More irritating than eczema?

MICHAEL. That was taken out of context . . .

REBECCA. Context? In what context would . . .

LUCIFER. You can see his point . . .

REBECCA. Sorry, who are you?

MICHAEL. They both think they're the father.

REBECCA. I thought Gary Goodman was the father?

LUCIFER. No, *I'm* the father.

GABRIEL. Er, I think you'll find . . .

LUCIFER. *Er, I think you'll find . . .*

MIA. He's Lucifer . . . a Fallen Angel, and he's Gabriel an . . . Archangel?

GABRIEL. Archangel, that's right.

REBECCA. They're . . . angels?

LUCIFER. Not any more.

MICHAEL. Of course they are, and she's the Virgin Mary, and Gary Goodman's a humble carpenter and they all came here via a little fucking donkey.

MIA. Oh, how very droll, Michael, well done.

REBECCA. . . . Angels . . . and why are they here again?

MIA. To fight over the soul of my unborn baby. Look, Rebecca don't worry about it, it's not your problem . . . Your problem is that you're a lying, deceitful, back-stabbing little cow, who is now going out with a lying, deceitful, back-stabbing little dickhead who has a hairy back and makes a stupid whistling noise through his nose when he sleeps, like there's a tiny elfin teapot stuck up there.

MICHAEL. I have sinus problems, you know that, thank you for drawing attention to it.

REBECCA. Look, I know I've not been totally straight with you but . . .

MIA. Not been totally straight? Rebecca, you've not been partially straight. In fact, I'd go so far as to say that you've been a circle . . .

GABRIEL. Look, people, let's all calm down, sit down. Lucie put the kettle on . . .

LUCIFER. You put the kettle on . . .

GABRIEL. Lucifer!

GABRIEL *gathers* MIA, MICHAEL *and* REBECCA *into a huddle to try and sort out their differences, they speak silently to one another.*

LUCIFER *turns to the audience.*

LUCIFER. Unbelievable!

He's so bloody high and mighty, every time I try to do something a bit different, fatty turns up to spoil the party. He just can't stand someone else being in the limelight for a bit. This was my time to shine, time for me to have a star and some wise men and some . . . shepherds.

You know, I don't know why I bother. I keep plugging away, trying to make a difference but nobody wants to listen. This world is going to Heaven and nobody wants to do a thing about it. You know, I try and I try, trying to save you people from eternity in that dull as dishwater place, but everything I do seems to get twisted and taken the wrong way.

Garden of Eden – you want an apple? Have an apple, it's called fruit, doctors recommend you have five portions a day, it'll help with your digestion . . . What, and now I'm the bad guy?

Garden of Gethsemane – you don't want to be crucified? Fair do's, who would? Let me help you out? Oh, and now suddenly I'm the scourge of all mankind.

OK, so maybe I should stay out of other people's gardens but I was just trying to help . . . People have such a warped perception of me and, well, if I'm honest, it can be quite upsetting at times.

You know, he has all these followers and all these songs about him . . . OK, so I have followers and songs but have you seen those people?

All the black nails and greasy hair, it creeps me out a bit if I tell you the truth.

I mean, I'm not a bad person . . .

But what can you do when they've got the Kingdom of Heaven PR machine blowing on full tilt?

I tell you, that bloody book will be the death of me . . . and the thing that gets me is that it's not even any good. Have you read the thing? Bloody hell, it's tedious, parts of it aren't even legible, but then it sells more than *Harry Potter*, go figure.

And does anybody want to listen to my side of the story?

For a religion that isn't supposed to judge, they were pretty quick to damn me.

I am the victim of a smear campaign. If I wanted to, I could write a book slagging them all off but you know what? Frankly, I'm better than that.

I've sat there for centuries while all these lies have been spread about me. I've kept a quiet, dignified silence in the firm belief that at some point the truth will out, taken the higher ground as it were but . . . while they continue to play dirty like this . . .

Getting upset.

I'm sorry, I'm sorry . . . You know, I liked it up there and whatever the book says, me and the big man got on well, there was a time when we were very close, but it was always 'Jesus this, Jesus that' . . . I gave that man the best years of my life and what thanks did I get?

Fallen Angel indeed . . . I didn't fall. I was pushed.

LUCIFER *flounces off to make the tea.*

The conversation between GABRIEL, MIA, MICHAEL *and* REBECCA *suddenly fades up again.*

GABRIEL (*as if midway through conversation*). . . . and it was the largest squirrel penis I'd ever seen.

They all laugh.

Beat.

GABRIEL *then checks to make sure* LUCIFER *is gone before continuing.*

Look, did you definitely have sex with this . . . Gary . . . ?

MICHAEL. . . . Goodman.

GABRIEL. Goodman.

REBECCA. I can't believe you had sex with Gary Goodman.

GABRIEL. Well, is it true . . . ?

MIA. I . . . well, I don't know . . .

GABRIEL. You don't know?

MIA. . . . I think so . . .

GABRIEL. . . . you *think* so?

MIA. Yes, I'm not sure, why does it matter?

GABRIEL. Why does it *matter*?

MIA. Yes. WHY DOES IT MATTER? Will you stop bloody repeating everything I say . . . ?

GABRIEL. It matters, missy, because we need to determine whether or not that little fella in there is the second coming or the spawn of the Devil . . .

MIA. Well, surely you should know . . . I thought you people knew *everything*. I mean, God must know who he impregnates . . . ?

In fact, he's supposed to be omnipresent, so surely he should know whether I had sex with Gary Goodman or not?

GABRIEL. I . . . well . . . that is a good point.

MIA. Well, hasn't he told you? I'd have thought if he'd sent you here to speak to me he'd at least have filled you in on the finer details.

GABRIEL. Well . . . I . . . you'd have thought, I mean . . . I'm sort of on a need-to-know basis.

MIA. You don't think this is something you need to know?

GABRIEL. Well, yes, I suppose it is . . .

MIA. So why don't we ask him?

GABRIEL. You can't just walk up to God and *ask* Him . . .

MIA. Why not?

GABRIEL. Well, you just can't . . .

REBECCA. Why not?

GABRIEL. . . . I . . .

REBECCA. So he just impregnates at will, a girl he barely even knows, then sends you down to sort out the mess?

GABRIEL. It's . . .

MICHAEL. . . . like some sort of evangelical rock star . . . A holy Mick Jagger with hundreds of kids at every port.

GABRIEL. Um . . . well, no, it's not quite . . .

MIA. . . . and then he sends you down here to try and sort things out for him . . . appease the burdened woman?

GABRIEL. I, no, look . . .

REBECCA. You're just kind of like a glorified PA really.

GABRIEL. Now hang on here, this isn't about me.

MIA. No, it's not . . .

GABRIEL (*beat*). Look, did you have sex with Gary Goodman or not?

There is a knock at the door . . . Beat, everyone looks confused. There is another knock, REBECCA *goes to the door and opens it. It is* GARY GOODMAN.

REBECCA. Oh my God!

MIA. Oh my God!

MICHAEL. Oh my God!

LUCIFER *walks in with a tray of tea and a packet of chocolate Hobnobs. He sees* GARY.

LUCIFER. Oh my God!

GABRIEL. Who's this now?

GARY. . . . I'm Gary Goodman . . .

GABRIEL. Oh . . . Oh my God . . .

GARY *looks a little shocked at this reaction. There is a long silence, he looks very nervous.*

GARY. OK . . . I . . . (*Turning to* MIA.) Look, I got your address off Friends Reunited, Matthew Parker had it, he said that Karen Denver had given it to him a couple of months ago because he wanted to invite you to some charity netball do he was organising . . .

MIA (*cutting him off, to* REBECCA). God, yeah, did you get one of those?

REBECCA. What?

MIA. Matthew Parker just sent me this random invite through the post for this netball thing.

MICHAEL. Shit, yeah, I remember that.

REBECCA. You didn't tell me about this. Did you go?

MIA. No . . .

Beat. Everyone looks back at a nervous GARY.

GARY. Right . . . so Matthew was the first person on the list to have it, so that's why it's taken me so long . . . a few people had your old address at Sumner Road. But obviously you've moved now, there's an Asian couple living there now, very nice . . .

There is silence, everyone is just staring at him.

. . . Look . . . (*To* MIA.) . . . could I, have a word . . . in private?

*He looks at the others who all are staring, they take the hint
and pretend to busy themselves.* GARY *moves in towards*
MIA. *The others listen in and react to the speech.*

I didn't want you to think I was a love 'em and leave 'em
type of guy, you know . . . a user . . . because I'm not . . .
I have the highest respect for birds . . . I love 'em, I know
I can come across as a bit of a high-flyer, someone with a
girl at every port . . .

But truth is . . .

I'm a virgin . . .

Well, I was, until you . . .

That night, God, it was like I was taken over by some
higher power or something . . .

Everyone looks at LUCIFER. *He shuffles uneasily and
mouths the word 'Lust'.*

. . . I just felt irresistible . . .

I mean, I always used to fancy you at school. If I'm honest,
those Valentines cards, with the question marks on them,
they were from me . . .

I was in love with you.

So when I saw you that night . . . and then we . . .

Well, it was like a dream come true.

I mean, I felt something inside me . . . and I know you did
too.

Look, what I'm trying to say is . . .

I think I'm in love with you . . .

Again . . .

Anyway, enough about me, boring, how have you been,
you're looking well, radiant . . .

You've been eating well, I see.

*Referencing the bump, he smiles, after a while the penny
drops.*

Oh my God, you're . . .

We're gonna have a . . .

I'm gonna be a . . .

MIA. No . . .

GARY. . . . on target first time! Back of the net!

MIA. Look, Gary . . . It's not yours . . .

GARY. What do you mean? It must be . . .

MIA. Trust me.

GARY. You don't have to lie to me, it's OK, I want a baby,
     I want *your* baby . . .

MIA. No, really, Gary, you don't want *this baby.*

GARY. I do, I'd never shirk my responsibility . . . Let's get
     married, we'll bring it up together . . . This is my baby, I
     know it is . . .

LUCIFER. It's not your baby, it's my baby.

GABRIEL. It's not your baby . . .

GARY. Oh . . . I . . . (*Looking at* LUCIFER.) . . . Sorry, haven't
     we met before?

LUCIFER. I don't think so.

GARY. I'm sure we have.

LUCIFER. No.

GARY. You look so familiar.

LUCIFER. I get that a lot . . . just one of those faces . . .

GARY. Right . . .

     Beat.

     So whose baby is it then?

GABRIEL. It's God's baby.

GARY. What?

MIA. Shut up, Gabriel.

GARY. Gabriel?

GABRIEL. Yes, I am the Angel Gabriel and this baby was immaculately conceived.

LUCIFER *yawns.*

GARY. I . . . you're the Angel Gabriel? But where are your wings?

GABRIEL. What is this obsession with wings . . . ? Look . . .

He grabs one of the mugs of tea and shows it to GARY.

Water . . . OK? Well, tea . . .

He waves his hand over it. There is the brief strain of a heavenly chorus.

. . . Wine . . .

You happy?

GARY *drinks it.*

GARY. It's wine . . . it's WINE! It's a miracle! A miracle!

LUCIFER. Give me a break.

MIA. Why wouldn't you do that for me?

GABRIEL. I'm not a performing seal . . .

GARY. Oh my God . . . I mean, gosh . . . I mean . . .

This is incredible, it's a sign . . .

You're here to save me, right? To save my soul? . . .
Because I had sex with her, before we were married . . .

GABRIEL. Er . . .

GARY. I'm sorry . . . I didn't want to, well, I did want to . . .
I . . . She tricked me . . . How can I ever be forgiven for my sins of the flesh?

GABRIEL. Er . . . right, sure . . . well, just go and spread the good word, you know . . . that sort of thing . . .

GARY. Yes, yes, spread the good word, that sort of thing, of course . . . I'll spread it, spread it wide . . . (*Noticing* MIA.) Oh, you and me . . . er . . . not going to work out . . . know that a part of me will always love you . . . Take care of that little fella, yeah?

He looks back to GABRIEL.

Spread the word!

GARY *smiles at everyone then steps forward to address the audience.*

GARY. Who'd have thought it, eh? Me and the Angel Gab . . .

MIA. Gary, what are you doing?

GARY. What, I was just . . .

MIA. No, Gary.

GARY. I just thought maybe . . .

He gestures to the audience.

MIA. No.

GARY. No? Just, it's kind of an insight into my . . .

MIA. Not going to happen.

GARY. . . . Right.

He looks to the others but they shake their heads. GARY *sighs, disappointed. He picks himself up to be jolly* GARY *again, almost parodying himself.*

OK then, guess I'll go spread the word then, yeah?

MIA. Goodbye Gary.

GARY. Spread the word . . .

He leaves awkwardly upstage right. Beat.

GABRIEL. So *that* was Gary Goodman, he seemed . . . nice.

MICHAEL *and* REBECCA *burst out laughing.*

MIA. Shut up.

MICHAEL *and* REBECCA *laugh again.*

LUCIFER. Dear me, Gabriel, having to resort to parlour tricks to recruit your new members now . . . ?

GABRIEL. I was simply telling him what the situation was . . . It got rid of him, didn't it . . . ?

LUCIFER. Unbelievable . . . Well, do you at least believe me now . . . ? I told you she'd had sex with him.

MICHAEL *and* REBECCA *laugh again.*

GABRIEL. Hmmm . . . Well, I suppose this does change things a bit. We just need to find some way of making sure of who the father is.

LUCIFER. Let's do a DNA test. It'll be just like *Trisha*!

GABRIEL. God doesn't *do* DNA.

MIA. I don't believe this, it's ridiculous, this whole thing is ridiculous, I've been practically celibate for the last year, how can I be pregnant and have three men all claiming to be the father; two of which, many people believe don't even exist?

GABRIEL. God moves in mysterious . . .

MIA. DON'T EVEN SAY IT! Talk amongst yourselves . . .

She steps forwards and addresses the audience.

So what do I do now? How does the modern woman cope with immaculate conception? What happened to pro-choice? You can't just invade a woman's body, like some sort of illegal occupation of a foreign state and then implant your own government without the consent of the citizens. You can't just break into a woman's most sacred sanctuary and fill her with a piece of your life. Stick it in the fridge to keep it cool, pop it in the oven 'til it's ready then take it out and serve it to the world. I'm not the Big Yellow Storage Company, I don't rent out space, I don't do babysitting, baby-growing . . . like a greenhouse, an empty vessel, somewhere to keep it warm and safe, to carry it and look after it, a means to an end, well, so what if the end justifies the means, I'm not talking about the bigger picture, the longer run, the greater good.

This is my place, my space, for me to use as I see fit, you can't just invade it without my permission, that completely negates my basic human rights, that's rape . . .

It's not my baby, I didn't ask for it, I don't want it, it just appeared . . .

I can't look after a baby . . . I can't look after myself . . . you can give me all the myrrh in the world, it won't make any difference.

I'm not a mother . . . I'm a daughter . . .

. . .

Anyway, how much of this baby is even mine? I mean, a baby is a mixture, a combination, a chemical reaction, two pieces merging together to create something new . . .

But how can that work . . . ?

It would take half my looks, half my traits . . . It might be scared of photocopiers like me, the Almighty can't be scared of photocopiers . . . or suffer from bad skin . . . or be allergic to peanuts, or be terrible at mathematics and home economics . . .

These aren't traits of the Almighty, signs of perfection, they're imperfections . . . human . . .

. . . and what if it isn't the Son of God but the Spawn of the Devil . . . my own little Damien . . . well, fuck that . . . why would I want one of them? Why would I want to bring up the leader of all things evil . . . ? What do I get out of that? Will he look after his mum in her old age? Will he bollocks, he's evil? All I'll get is an eternity of fire and brimstone for harbouring a known criminal for nine months . . .

Upside-down crosses everywhere, crows, dogs, serpents, rogue priests turning up at my house in sweat-drenched robes . . .

I can't be doing with all that.

I'll be targeted by extremists, worshipped by weirdos, canonised, vilified, terrorised, a martyr, a saint . . .

I'll be re-opening old wounds,

Re-emphasising the gulf that lies between beliefs,

Refreshing the reasons for wars and genocide,

I'll be giving people justification for the unjustifiable . . .

. . .

. . . and I didn't even have a choice . . . but then you never do . . .

Beat. She turns to the others.

What if I chose not to have the baby?

LUCIFER. What?

GABRIEL. You can't, you don't even know whose it is yet?

MIA. What difference does it make? Either way will lead to an apocalypse and half of the population being damned to eternal suffering?

I don't want to be responsible for that.

GABRIEL. But He's your saviour.

MIA. No, he's *your* saviour, the saviour of *your* establishment, a popularity boost before the leadership is decided, he'll help you more than he'll help us. We're not perfect, none of us are perfect, we'll be left behind.

GABRIEL. You can be forgiven.

MIA. What if we don't want to be forgiven? What if we don't think we've actually done anything wrong? Salvation shouldn't come with conditions, surely that misses the point?

LUCIFER. Now *that*, Gabriel, is what I call seeing the light . . .

MIA. What is it with you people? The moment someone shows disillusionment in one camp, you automatically assume they've devoted themselves to the other. Did you ever consider that maybe I don't care for either of you?

Beat.

REBECCA. . . . . Who wants tea?

MICHAEL. Yeah, are all those Hobnobs gone?

GABRIEL. Lucifer was going through them earlier like they were going out of fashion.

LUCIFER. I need the sugar for my diabetes.

MIA. There's another packet in the cupboard but they might be dark chocolate.

MICHAEL. I don't understand why you always buy dark chocolate biscuits.

REBECCA. Dark chocolate is better for you, it's less addictive and contains a lot of antioxidants . . .

Beat. Everyone muses over this interesting nugget of information.

LUCIFER. We still haven't come to any sort of conclusion?

REBECCA. What sort of conclusion do you want?

GABRIEL. A suitable one.

MIA. A suitable conclusion would be for me to realise that I cannot have this baby and then to dispose of it by going to the kitchen, pulling out a rusty old bread knife from the drawer and stabbing myself through the stomach . . .

Or throwing myself down several flights of stairs, landing in a crumpled mess at the bottom . . .

Or striding proudly into a lake as the ice-cold water gobbles me up and sends my billowing dress flowing outwards across the water, spreading like a flower opening until the water soaks through and the weight of it drags me helplessly to the bottom. Something dramatic like that would be *suitable*, though when is anything ever suitable . . .

Most likely I'll just go to my doctors and get him to suck it out painlessly, then cry a lot, feel guilty, drink a lot and cry some more.

MICHAEL. That all sounds rather bleak.

MIA. It does, doesn't it . . .

MICHAEL. So how about that tea?

MIA. Yes, anyone else?

LUCIFER. I'll have a coffee if you've got it, black.

GABRIEL. I'll take a coffee too but only if you've got a decaf.

REBECCA. Tea is fine.

> MIA *goes to leave the room, the phone rings, everyone looks at it. After a few rings it goes to answer machine.*

PHONE. Hello, this is Dr Wells, I'm calling about the results of your tests. As we suspected, you are definitely pregnant . . .

. . . quite far gone it seems, nearly seven months.

. . . It would be good if you could come back in so that we can discuss your options . . .

I know the pregnancy wasn't planned . . .

. . . as you may know the legal limit for termination is twenty-four weeks and well, as I said, you appear to be at least six months gone which may mean that termination is no longer an option . . . I appreciate it's a lot to take in so I'll leave you to it now. Come in and see me in the next week and hey, send my congratulations to the father . . . you're going to have a baby!

> *Everyone stares at the phone in silence, they look at* MIA. *She calmly heads to the door.*

GABRIEL. Where are you going?

MIA. I'm going to the kitchen . . .

> *She exits upstage left, silence. The characters left on stage take their chorus masks from the hatstand and put them on. The dramatic chorus music plays.*

CHORUS.
> And so we near the climax of our tale
> Our heroine leaves the fracas, sick and pale
> Who the father is we do not know

But nevertheless inside a babe doth grow.
One way he'll grow to save those who believe
But damn all those who don't with no reprieve.
The other way will see him lead from Hell
So neither option really works out well.
Faced with such a future she soon knew
That there was only one thing she could do
And so into her kitchen she did go
Determined not to let this creature grow
And grabbing firm the rusty old bread knife
She prepared herself to take her life.
She raised the weapon high above her head
Then plunged the knife inside and fell down dead
The blood flowed like a river through the . . .

MIA *re-enters with a tray of teas.*

MIA. OK, Gabriel, I'm out of decaf so I've done you a tea, I . . .

She notices the CHORUS.

What's going on?

CHORUS.
You were supposed to go and take your life
To stab yourself with the rusty old bread knife?

MIA. Excuse me? Why would I do that?

CHORUS.
Er . . . To stop your unborn baby being born
And ushering in a biblical new dawn?

MIA. Whoa whoa, wait a second, I'm not going to kill myself.
What, just because I've been knocked up? It's not my fault,
and if I was going to do it, I certainly wouldn't do it with a
rusty old bread knife . . .

CHORUS. But you said . . .

MIA. I know what I said . . . I said that that would be suitable,
I didn't say I was going to do it, bloody hell! We don't do
things like that these days. I'm not going to pluck out my
eyes or hang myself from the ceiling of a cave, we're a lot
more civilised than that . . .

CHORUS.
But what about the ending of this story,
Do you not wish to die in a blaze of glory?

MIA. No! . . . And besides, this is not the end, there isn't an
end, things don't just stop . . . this is just the part you
happen to be telling . . .

CHORUS (*they think for a moment, then continue*).
So are you saying you're going to have the baby?

MIA. Maybe . . .

CHORUS. Maybe?

MIA. Yes, maybe . . . that's what I said. For goodness' sake,
will you stop talking like that, all this bloody unison,
rhyming couplet nonsense, it's not even a proper form of
verse, is it? What's the pentameter?

CHORUS.
I . . . We . . . we speak as one for that is how we . . .

We're here to, I mean . . . What I'm trying to say is . . .

MIA. This is ridiculous, stop it!

CHORUS. But . . .

MIA. Stop it . . . take those stupid masks off . . .

The CHORUS *look at each other and slowly and
embarrassedly take off their masks, all except* GABRIEL
who keeps his on.

They look at MIA *sheepishly.*

MIA. What are you doing . . . ? Your teas are over there . . .

GABRIEL. The chorus drank their teas and . . .

MICHAEL *hits* GABRIEL *on the arm,* GABRIEL
*awkwardly takes his mask off. They move over to the teas
shamefacedly and drink.*

MIA. So here it is . . . not the end of my story but the
beginning.

What happens next?

I could have the baby, who's to say it's going to follow in its father's footsteps . . . ? It may not want to be a Christ . . . or an anti-Christ.

I could just bring it up normally, nurture versus nature, give it a choice . . .

If there's any choice to give.

Perhaps I'm just part of a prophecy?

And my decisions have already been decided.

Sounds like an easy way out, but then what's the alternative . . . ?

That fate is a fiction?

That nothing is certain,

That nothing means anything,

That there's nowhere else to go,

That *this* is it?

Suddenly the stage is bathed with bright light. We hear a deafening noise almost like a heavenly chorus. Everyone walks downstage and stares up into the light – as if looking out of the window.

GABRIEL. It's happening, the baby is bringing light to the world. It's a sign!

MICHAEL. It's not a sign, it's a helicopter . . . they've got cameras!

REBECCA *grabs the remote control and switches the television on. (Note: the television can be the audience, so the cast all huddle downstage staring out. Alternatively, an onstage television could be used.)*

TV (NEWSREADER). . . . And now we're going live to our reporter who's outside the house . . .

TV (REPORTER). Yes, we're outside the apartment building where inside it is alleged the second coming is about to take place. As you can see, quite a crowd has gathered, here with me now is the man who first broke the story . . . Gary Goodman.

MIA, GABRIEL, MICHAEL, LUCIFER *and* REBECCA *all react.*

TV (GARY). Hi yes, I was there and it's all pretty amazing, the Angel Gabriel was there and he had this tea which he turned to wine and . . .

They look at GABRIEL *unimpressed.*

. . . well, he told me to spread the good word . . . to tell everyone . . .

He's coming . . . HE'S COMING!

TV (REPORTER). Thanks, Gary . . . Now I know it may seem beyond comprehension but if this does turn out to be true, we could be witnessing the biggest news story we've ever seen . . . it would truly change the world . . .

REBECCA *changes the channel; we hear another news broadcast covering the story, then another and another, each joining in over the top of each other, building.*

Foreign language news broadcasts start coming in: French, German, American, Spanish, Arabic, etc., as news spreads around the world until we can barely hear above the din of all the news reports.

During this, the lights slowly fade, leaving the cast in silhouette with just a flicker from the television.

Suddenly the noise stops. Blackout.

Beat.

We hear a baby cry.

Moments later, a second baby joins in.

End of play.